SO-CTA-589

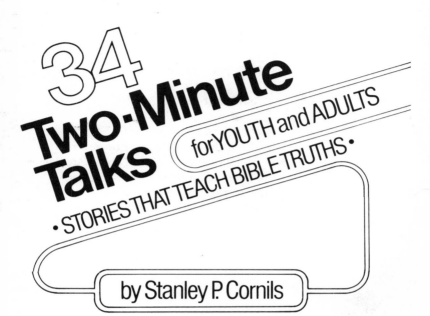

34 Two-Minute Talks

for YOUTH and ADULTS

• STORIES THAT TEACH BIBLE TRUTHS •

by Stanley P. Cornils

STANDARD PUBLISHING
Cincinnati, Ohio   2883

DEDICATION

This book is dedicated
to
Kristie and Kevin Cornils,
two of my grandchildren
who helped me write it,
to a host of children in the congregations
where I have ministered and shared these stories,
and to the many friends who encouraged
me to put them in print.

Unless otherwise indicated, all Scripture quotations are taken from the HOLY BIBLE: NEW INTERNATIONAL VERSION, Copyright © 1973, 1978 by the International Bible Society. Used by permission of Zondervan Bible Publishers.

Sharing the thoughts of his own heart, the author may express views that are not entirely consistent with those of the publisher.

ISBN 0-87239-868-4

Copyright © 1985 by Stanley P. Cornils, Vallejo, California. Published by the STANDARD PUBLISHING Company, Cincinnati, Ohio. A division of STANDEX INTERNATIONAL Corporation. Printed in U.S.A.

CONTENTS

WHY YOU HAD TO DO IT

Louis Cassels

PHIL 2:6-8 ...MADE IN HUMAN LIKENESS...

Once upon a time, there was a man who looked upon Christmas as a lot of humbug. He wasn't a Scrooge. He was a kind and decent person, generous to his family and upright in all his dealings with other men. But he didn't believe all that stuff about incarnation that churches proclaim at Christmas. And he was too honest to pretend that he did.

"I am truly sorry to distress you," he told his wife, who was a faithful churchgoer, "but I simply cannot understand this claim that God became man. It doesn't make any sense to me."

One Christmas Eve, as usual, his wife and children went to church for the midnight service. He declined to accompany them. "I'd feel like a hypocrite," he explained. "I'd rather stay at home. But I'll wait up for you."

Shortly after his family drove away in the car, snow began to fall. He went to the window and watched the flurries getting heavier and heavier. "If we must have Christmas," he thought, "it's nice to have a white one." He went back to his chair by the fireside and began to read the newspaper.

A few minutes later, he was startled by a thudding sound. It was quickly followed by another, then another. He thought that someone must be throwing snowballs at his living-room window. When he went to the front door to investigate, he found a flock of birds huddled miserably in the snow. They had been caught in the storm, and in a desperate search for shelter had tried to fly through his window.

"I can't let these poor creatures lie here and freeze," he thought. "But how can I help them?" Then he remembered the barn where the children's pony was stabled. It would provide a warm shelter. He put on his coat and boots and tramped through the deepening snow to the barn. He opened the door wide and turned on a light. But the birds didn't come in. "Food will bring them in," he thought. So he hurried back to the house for bread crumbs, which he sprinkled on the snow to make a trail into the barn. To his dismay, the birds ignored the bread crumbs and continued to flop

5

around helplessly in the snow. He tried shooing them into the barn by walking around and waving his arms. They scattered in every direction except toward the warm, lighted barn.

"They find me a strange and terrifying creature," he said to himself, "and I can't seem to think of any way to let them know they can trust me. If only I could be a bird myself for a few minutes, perhaps I could lead them to safety...."

Just at that moment, the church bells began to ring. He stood silently for a while, listening to the bells pealing the glad tidings of Christmas. Then he sank to his knees in the snow. "Now I understand," he whispered. "Now I see why You had to do it."

Reprinted by permission of United Press International.

6

THE BLACK BEETLE AND THE DRAGON FLY

Cecil B. deMille

Scripture Text: 1 Corinthians 15

Cecil B. deMille was not only a great movie producer; he also was a man who had a great Christian faith. On the evening of February 13, 1939, as a part of the Lux Radio Theatre broadcast, he shared with his audience how he had been inspired to write the play of that evening: The Return of Peter Grimm.

We flash back to the time when David Belasco commissioned me to get an idea for a new play for David Warfield. I went to Maine loaded down with pencils, paper, and enthusiasm. But ideas often come slowly and the inspiration which I hoped would come like a bolt of summer lightning failed to strike.

Then one day, lying in a canoe very close to shore, I was reading a book when a big black beetle came out of the water, crawled up on the gun'l and sat there blinking at me. And while he sat, I noticed a score of his relations grubbing in the muddy bottom of the lake. I felt rather sorry for them—those lowly creatures that might never know any other world except gloom and mud and water.

Under the heat of the sun, the beetle proceeded to die. Then a strange thing happened. His glistening black shell cracked down the back. Out of it came a shapeless mass, whose hideousness was transformed, as I watched, into beautiful brilliantly colored life. Out of the mass gradually unfolded four iridescent wings from which the sunlight flashed a thousand colors. The wings spread wide, as if in worship. The blue-green body took shape. Before my eyes had occurred a metamorphosis—the transformation into another world—of a hideous beetle to a gorgeous dragonfly, which started dipping and soaring over the water. But the body it had left behind still clung to the gun'l of my canoe.

And while the dragonfly happily explored its wonderful new world—darting in an instant over a space that a short time before would have taken it months to crawl—the other beetles still plodded and lumbered below in the mire. I wondered if they were conscious of the glorious creature flitting over their heads or if the dragonfly, which so recently had been one of them, could look down and see and understand its fellow beetles crawling along the bottom of the lake. I had witnessed what seemed to me a miracle. Out of the mud had come a beautiful new life. And the thought came to me that if the Creator works such wonders with the lowliest of creatures, what may be in store for the human spirit? But I didn't let that distract me then, because the beetle had given me the idea for the play—a play about a man who died and returned.... And ever since that day in Maine, a long time ago, I have had a deep, abiding faith in immortality. Why have any doubt that there is a hereafter?

Used by permission of Lever Brothers Company, New York, New York.

MY DADDY CAME HOME TODAY

"Where are the other nine?" (Luke 17:17).

It was during the dark days of World War II. The Netherlands had fallen, the Belgian plain had been overrun, and France was being taken. The British Expeditionary Force had been sent to assist the beleagured French and Belgian forces, but with little effect. Late in May, 1940, the British found their mission hopeless, and the only way out was the port of Dunkirk.

Over 338,000 British, French, and Belgian troops were hemmed in at Dunkirk, without sufficient Navy vessels to rescue them. The weary Allies sought shelter amid the sand dunes while the Nazi planes sprayed them with machine-gun fire. It looked as though their cause was hopeless unless God worked a miracle.

Between May 26 and June 4, perhaps as many as 650 boats of all descriptions, from British Navy vessels to lowly fishing boats, participated in one of the most daring—if not miraculous—rescues ever. With help from the Royal Air Force and Hitler's decision not to use tanks at Dunkirk, this rag-tag armada succeeded in getting the Allies out of Dunkirk before the Nazis were able to occupy the port.

In England, a minister noticed a small boy come into the church sanctuary and kneel to pray. It was not a Sunday or any other special day, just an ordinary weekday. He knelt for so long a time that the minister began to wonder about him.

When the boy finally arose to leave, the minister asked, "Do you come here often to pray?"

"I have come four times in the last five days," he replied.

"Do you have someone fighting at Dunkirk?" asked the perceptive minister.

"Yes, my daddy," the boy replied. "But he came home today; so I came to church to thank God for getting him home safely."

Too often, we are like the nine lepers in the story from Luke's Gospel. When we get what we want from God, we forget to thank Him. How could we ever be so ungrateful?

9

Prayer is not always asking God for something, or pleading for some kind of miracle. One of the most beautiful parts of prayer is the coming back, as did the man in the New Testament story, and as did the English lad, to give thanks to God.

Someone has suggested that we would more often have results for which to thank God if we more often gave thanks for the results that we do get!

ISRAEL HAS TWO SEAS

There are two seas in the land of Israel. The Jordan River flows into the Sea of Galilee in the north. Its waters are clear, fresh, and blue. The fish that are caught here provide a livelihood for many people. Trees and other vegetation line its shores. Many living creatures make their homes here. The area is filled with beauty and life.

At the southern end, there is another sea: the Dead Sea, which is forty-seven miles long and about ten miles wide. It lies 1286 feet below sea level—the lowest body of water in the world. Nineteen billion cubic feet of water flow into the Dead Sea every year from the Jordan River and other smaller streams.* In some places, it is more than 1000 feet deep. The water is more than five times as salty as ordinary sea water—so salty, in fact, that the human body floats on the surface. There is no life in the Dead Sea, except for a few kinds of microbes. Ocean fish planted here soon die. The Dead Sea is a picture of desolation and gloom, looking as if the curse of God rested on the region.

What makes the difference between these two bodies of water? All the water that flows into the Sea of Galilee also flows south into the Dead Sea—the receiving and giving go on in equal measure. Every drop the Sea of Galilee receives, it gives. It gives and lives. But the Dead Sea has no outlet. The only water it loses is that which is lost by evaporation. Every drop it gets, it keeps. One might say it is shrewd, keeping to itself all that it receives. The Dead Sea is a symbol of selfishness.

In the parable of the talents (Matthew 25:14-30) and elsewhere, Jesus taught that we are responsible for how we use what is given to us. He instructed his disciples, "Freely you have received, freely give" (Matthew 10:8).

There are two seas in the land of Israel. There are two kinds of people in the world. Which kind are you?

*Encylopedia Britannica, 1980, Vol. 5, p. 525.

THAT IS *A*

Lloyd Douglas, the famous author, one day happened into the studio of a friend, an elderly violin teacher. This man had a plain and simple wisdom that was always refreshing.

"What's the good word today?" Douglas inquired.

The old man laid down his violin and struck the tuning fork that hung from a silken cord. "That, my friend is *A*. It was *A* yesterday; it will be *A* tomorrow, and it will be *A* until the end of time. The soprano upstairs may warble off key; the tenor next door may be flat on his high notes; and the piano in the next room may be out of tune, but that, my friend, is *A*."

When an orchestra is preparing to give a concert, every instrument must be tuned. Generally the pianist strikes *A* and everyone tunes to that. After playing each main selection, the musicians carefully retune. If they neglect to do this, their music becomes discordant and unpleasant to hear.

Jesus was not in tune with the people of His day. He did not live and believe as so many of them did because He was attuned to the will of His Father. One day He told his disciples: "My food is to do the will of Him who sent me" (John 4:34). This is the reason so many of His teachings seemed different and revolutionary. He taught that we should love our enemies; and that is not easy, because it is more natural to love our friends and hate our enemies. He also said, "It is more blessed to give than to receive" (Acts 20:35). Most of us are more in tune with our human nature, which is inclined to be selfish rather than generous.

If we would be His faithful and obedient disciples, His perfect example is the *A* to which we should tune our attitudes and actions. What a different world ours would be if everyone were tuned to the *A* of our Lord's teaching and example. That is the *A* for us.

THE WINDOW AND THE MIRROR

As a part of their folklore, our Jewish friends have a story about a window and a mirror that contains a lesson we should never forget.

Once there was a very rich man who spent most of his time thinking of himself and counting his money. Sitting in his counting room, he would let the silver and gold coins flow through his fingers onto the table like a cascading waterfall. Their ring as they hit the marble top of the table or as they jostled one against the other was music to his ears. He probably was the most wealthy man of his country. He ate fine foods, had expensive clothing, lived in a big beautiful house, and was waited on by many servants. He was happy with his lot in life.

Because he was selfish, he had no interest in what went on in the world outside his house. He had no time for what happened in his city or interest in what the people's needs were. Yet every day scores of people, many of them poor and needy, passed by his window. But he never looked through the window to notice them or their needs; he heard only the clink of his coins. He was a miser.

But one day he began to worry about himself. He had not been sleeping well lately, nor did he enjoy eating as before. Even counting his money no longer gave him the same satisfaction. Something must be wrong, he thought. So he sent a message asking the wise man to come and visit him.

After the wise man had arrived and asked why he had been summoned, the rich man told him of his problems. "Please give me your blessing," he pleaded, "so I can find pleasure in life again."

The wise man thought a moment; then he took him by the arm and led him to the window overlooking the street. They stood silently for a few moments.

"What do you see as you look through the window?" the wise man asked.

"I see people," replied the rich man.

"What kind of people?" asked the wise man.

13

"I see that poor woman pulling the shawl over her head to protect her from the cold. I see the peddler selling vegetables from his pushcart. I see children playing. I see a little boy helping a crippled lady across the street." He was fascinated by what he was seeing through the window.

Then the wise man led him across the room and placed him before a mirror and asked, "Now, what do you see?"

"I see myself," he replied.

The wise man asked him to be seated. Then he took the mirror from the wall and turned it over to show its silvered back. He said, "In the window there is glass, and in the mirror there is glass. Look through the window and you see people and their needs. But add a bit of silver and you have created a mirror in which you see only yourself."

From that day on, the miser was changed. He not only spent time looking through his window, but went out among the people and made himself one of them. He helped many of them with gifts of money. Some he helped in other ways. He joined the human race, as we would say. In a very short time, his problems of worry and sleeplessness and loss of appetite all disappeared.

"Each of you should look not only to your own interests, but also to the interests of others" (Philippians 2:4).

CALAMITY JANE

One sunny afternoon, two men, both interested in golf, were strolling through a garden, enjoying the afternoon as they chatted together. Eventually they wandered into an old shed in one corner of the garden—a storage house for tools, furniture, and a lot of other things that had outgrown their usefulness.

Looking around this array of junk and castoffs, one of the men spied something of interest on a shelf and inquired: "What's that on the shelf, pal?"

"Just an old golf club," replied his host. He reached up and took the rusty old putter from the shelf and handed it to his friend, who began gripping the handle and getting the feel of the club as he swung it a few times over his head.

"You know?" he said. "I like the feel of this. Mind if I keep it? From the looks of it, you have no further interest in it, judging from all the rust that has gathered on it."

"Take it," said his friend. "I threw it up there several years ago, and haven't thought of it since. That club brought me so much trouble and misfortune that I named it 'Calamity Jane.' One day I was way off on my putting and that club kept bringing me bad luck. When I got home, I just put it out of my sight, up on the shelf. There it's been for two or three years, forgotten and unmourned. It's no good. If you want it, take it, but don't blame me if you lose games trying to putt with that old iron."

Not long after that conversation, one of the most famous putts in the history of golfing was made with that putter. It happened on the eighteenth green of St. Andrews when with it, its new owner, Bobby Jones, won the Open Championship of Great Britain. He then followed that victory by winning the U.S. National Open Championship the same year. He was the first player ever to win both championships in the same year. This Bobby Jones did with a castoff and rusty old putter, "Calamity Jane."

What made the difference? The old putter was being played in the hands of a master golfer. Whose hands are holding and guiding your life? God wants to do something great with your life, but you must be surrendered to His hand.

TRADEMARKS

"The disciples were first called Christians at Antioch" (Acts 11:26).

Trademark is a familiar word to most people. It is a word that denotes a product that is manufactured and sold by a certain company. The trademark is registered with the United States Patent Office, and it is against the law for any other firm to use it. Sometimes we see the words, "Non-genuine without this trademark," printed or stamped upon an article or product. The trademark is a guarantee of genuineness.

When I say, "Coca Cola," what is it that quickly comes to your mind? Yes, a very familiar and delicious soft drink. This trademark is so well known that in a recent survey, 99% of the people asked were able to identify it correctly. Some other familiar trademarks are Thermos, Mimeograph, and Xerox. At one time, each of these products was associated only with the one company that invented, manufactured, and sold it. But down through the years, other companies have made similar products, and the name of the popular original has been applied to the copies. Before the competition came on the scene, *Coke* always meant *Coca Cola,* but nowadays *coke* may mean any cola flavored soft drink. Legally, *Coke* is still *Coca Cola,* but in common usage, it may be any cola. *Thermos* may mean any kind of container that will keep a liquid either hot or cold. Only the DuPont company may use the trademark *Thermos,* but people will always call the copies thermos, too. *Mimeograph* can mean most any brand of stencil and ink duplicator, but the fact remains that the trademark *Mimeograph* belongs to and can be used only by the A.B. Dick Company. *Xerox* is a trademark of a photocopying machine made by the Xerox Corporation. When we say that we are going to Xerox a copy, we actually mean we are going to photocopy it, unless we are really going to use a Xerox machine. You see, the trademarks have become so well known that their names have slipped into everyday language and lost their distinctive trademark value.

Almost two thousand years ago in the city of Antioch, the followers of Christ were first nicknamed "Christians" because their lives told the world that they were followers of Christ. This name became the trademark of everyone who had taken Christ as Savior and followed His teachings. The early Christians were people in whose lives Jesus had complete control. At least, it was true of most of them. But down through the years, something happened to the meaning of the word *Christian*. To many people today, the word *Christian* stands for anyone who goes to church; or who is not a Jew, a Mohammedan, a Buddhist, or an atheist; or just someone who always obeys the law and lives a good, clean life. Let's try to live true to our trademark. Our lives should remind others of our Christ.

OUR UNFINISHED WORLD

"Be fruitful and increase in number; fill the earth and subdue it" (Genesis 1:28).

God is all-powerful, but there are some things that He chooses not to do without man's help. He told our first parents to "subdue" the earth. That meant man was to work to make it a better world. Man was expected to contribute to its progress and completeness.

It should not surprise us that when God placed man on the earth, He did not give him a book of instructions about the world, nor an answer book to the how and why of things. Also, He did not give him a copy of the laws of nature and the universe, the multiplication table, or the alphabet. Man was going to have to find these things out on his own. This is one way we fulfill the "subdue" part of God's command.

Man cannot create anything as God created—in the sense of making something out of nothing—but he can create by taking what already exists and improving it. The little wild rose that grows in the pasture and on the hedge rows is a lovely flower, but it can not be compared with the scores of beautiful roses that grow in our gardens. You see, botanists, the scientists who deal with plants, started with the wild rose and over a period of many years developed the many varieties we have today. So it is with most of our fruits, vegetables, nuts, and domesticated animals.

Electricity has been in the atmosphere since the beginning of time, but man had to discover it and find ways of harnessing it so it would serve him and make his work easier. The principle of the wheel was always in the material world, but man probably took thousands of years to discover it and learn how he could make that principle work for him. Atomic energy and atomic power were present on the day of creation, but it took man thousands of years to find it, and only in the lifetime of some older people of today has man learned how to use it.

So much still needs to be discovered and done. Our world is yet

18

a long way from being subdued. We have not conquered wars; we have not mastered many of our diseases; we still have prejudices and ignorance in the world; and about one-half of the people of the world never get enough to eat.

Of course, God could solve all these problems for us in the wink of an eye, but He isn't going to. He has turned the management of the world over to man, and each one of us is expected to put forth our own efforts to help make our world a better world to the glory of God. There is something each of us can do to His glory, and God is depending on us to do something for our world while we are here.

No doubt you have heard of Antonio Stradivari, the famous maker of violins of the late sixteen and early seventeen hundreds. The instruments he made are worth thousands of dollars each. Their quality, tone, and beauty are the finest in the world. Here is what is supposed to be a true story of what happened one day in his studio:

A group of musicians was visiting him, and they were permitted to see, handle, and play some of these fine instruments. They were ecstatic in their praise. It all ended up with their blessing God and praising Him for producing such fine instruments. Antonio was a bit pushed out of shape because God seemed to be getting all the credit for a violin which Antonio had made with his own hands.

He was not about to be left without some credit; so, with a rather pompous and challenging voice, but with a twinkle in his eye, he said to them: "But you must remember that without Antonio, God does not make Stradivari violins."

Exactly!

Without your help, some things in this world aren't going to get done. God gives to each one of us the challenge of a very big job, a job so big that He is not going to do it alone. He needs our help.

LIBERATED LIKENESS

"... until Christ is formed in you" (Galatians 4:19).

You don't have to be a student of the arts to know a sculptor is a person who works with a hammer and chisel to carve an image or scene on stone or other material. Someone once said, however, that sculpture effects its aim by the removal of parts. While we would agree that this is an overly simple way of describing how it is done, the statement is 100% true. It's almost like the reply of a little fellow in grade school, who, when his teacher asked him how he would sculpt an elephant, replied, "I'd get a big piece of marble or granite; then I would take a hammer and chisel and chip away everything that doesn't look like an elephant."

Gutzon Borglum, the renowned sculptor of our century, who carved the four great presidents at the Mount Rushmore National Memorial in South Dakota, very much agreed with this. When people asked him how he did it, he replied: "They were there all the time. All I did was to chisel away the unnecessary granite so people could see them."

Have you seen this gigantic sculpture? If you haven't, I hope that some day you will. It is an impressive sight. Mr. Borglum worked on these four giant faces off and on for fourteen years. In 1941, he died at the age of seventy, just nine months before they were completed. His son, Lincoln, who had worked with him on the project, finished them in November of that year. These gigantic faces are five hundred feet above the base of the mountain, and are between fifty and seventy feet in height. Most of the work was done from scaffolding and with jackhammers.

Mr. Borglum had a great knowledge of the structure, strengths, and weaknesses of granite, which helped him meet many of the baffling difficulties he encountered in the course of his work. While he was finishing Lincoln's cheek, a reddish substance appeared on the granite. He had to find what caused it and how to remedy it because he didn't want "honest Abe" to appear to be blushing. He also had to turn the head of Jefferson slightly because of the inferior stone between his cheek and his nose.

20

In very much the same way, Christ is trying to perfect His image in us so that the world will be reminded of Him when they have dealings with us. Just like Mr. Borglum, Jesus has His problems with us. He knows all about our weaknesses, and yet He goes on working in our lives. When He was in the world, He chose some very unpromising characters to be His followers. Ever since, He has been making saints out of very unlikely and unsaintly people.

In his letter to the Christians in Galatia, the apostle Paul tells them he was having birth pains "until Christ be formed in you." He wanted to be sure that they lived and acted in such a way that the world would see Jesus in their lives. This is really the task of the church today, to help the world see the image of our living Lord in us. Everything our church does or ought to be doing should have this as its end and goal. Our work is not just to tell people about our Lord, but to show Him to them in our lives.

COUNT YOUR BLESSINGS

As we grow older, we come to see and understand the difference between our wants and our needs. The needs are those things that we say are necessary for us to get along in life, such as food, clothing, a home to live in, family, friends, health, education, and enough money to get by on. Our wants are the things we would like to have in addition to our needs. We might call them the frosting on the cake.

Even though the needs of most of us are quite well satisfied, we sometimes spend too much time looking at the wants and forget that we possess far more than the bare necessities of life if we would but take stock of what we do have and enjoy it. In other words, we should count our blessings, name them one by one.

Not very many years ago, there was an Indian chief who had a little farm in Oklahoma. On this farm he raised sheep and enough food to provide for his family. Their needs were satisfied. Then, one day, oil was discovered on his property; wells were drilled, pumps were installed, and the oil was being harvested. In the course of years, the chief became a very wealthy man. But unlike most of us, he did not use any of the money that came from his oil royalties. He still lived in his old house, wore the same kind of clothes, and drove the same car as before the oil had been discovered. He continued to live as a poor farmer who had to count every penny at least twice before he spent it. He didn't even buy new furniture for his home. He lived only on the income from his flock of sheep. The money from the oil was all deposited in the local bank.

Late in the summer of almost every year, he would go to the bank and tell his troubles to the banker, who had come to know and understand him very well through the years. And this was his tale of woe: "Grass all gone; sheep all sick; water holes all dried up. Me very poor man."

Of course, his banker knew that the story as he told it was really not true. The chief was making a mistake in looking only at one source of his wealth. The banker knew just what he needed, and it wasn't more money. He would take him into the vault where the money was kept and put the Indian's bags of money, much of it in silver dollars, on the table. Then he would go away, leaving the chief to count and stack his wealth.

In about an hour, the chief would call for the banker to come and lock it all up again. Then with a very descriptive gesture of contentment, he hooked his thumbs around the suspenders of his overalls, and as though he had not a care in the world he proudly reported to his banker friend: "Grass all very green; sheep all very healthy; water holes all full of water. Me very rich Indian."

What changed the story? If you look into the wrong end of a telescope, what you see will be very narrowed and small. But if you look through the proper end, what you see will be very much and very large. Let's look the right way and see just how much God really has blessed us!

BE CAREFUL HOW YOU SAY IT

"Speaking the truth in love" (Ephesians 4:15).

There will come times in your life, as there probably already have, when someone feels compelled to make a criticism of you to your face. No matter how many years we live, criticism will always be difficult to accept. But we can grow and improve by accepting honest criticism. Most of the time, criticism hurts because we know it's true, and we are convicted by it. There will be many times when you will think to yourself after someone has found fault with you: "But there must have been a better way of saying it."

You will also find that there are a few very choice people who can offer criticism in such a way that we do not become angry or hurt. One way of doing this is to give first a word of praise, then proceed with the criticism, and then try to end with a word of sincere encouragement. We might call this the sugar coating on the bitter pill.

There is an old story about a king in India who had a strange and troubling dream one night. Rightly or wrongly, he believed that dreams have a meaning. So he called his wise men to hear his dream and tell him what it meant.

When they were assembled before him, the king related his dream in a troubled voice: "Last night I dreamed that all of my teeth fell out. I'm afraid that something dreadful is going to happen to me."

For a while, the wise men looked silently at each other. "Speak up!" cried the king. "Can't any of you tell me the meaning of my dream?"

One man stepped forward, bowed reverently before the king and said, "Oh, my gracious king, your dream has a sad meaning. It means that all your relatives will die—your parents, your brother, your sister, and your wife, and you will be left alone."

For a moment the king was silent. Then he became angry and shouted at the wise man, "How dare you give such a meaning to my dream? I do not believe you. You are not a wise man," and with that he instructed a soldier to take the unfortunate man away and give him a hundred lashes with a whip.

Then the king turned to the other wise men and said, "Now, who can tell me the real meaning of my dream. Speak! Or I will have you beheaded."

One of them timidly and with bowed head, stepped forward and said, "You are very fortunate, my king. Your dream has in it the promise of much happiness. You will live and rule over your people for many years. You will enjoy good health and a long, long life. You will live longer than any of your relatives—your parents, your brother, your sister, and your wife."

The king's face lit up with gladness as he said, "That is a good interpretation of my dream; here are a hundred gold pieces for giving me such good news."

One wise man whispered to another, "What happened? That's the same thing the first man told him. He received a hundred lashes, while this one received a hundred pieces of gold."

"True," answered his friend, "but there is more than one way of telling a thing."

Try to remember this when you feel the need to criticize someone. Choose your words in such a way that your friend will not be angry with you, but will love you and be helped by your remarks. Make certain that your love shows through. You might even first ask yourself, "How would I feel if someone said this to me in this way?"

"Speak the truth in love."

THANK GOD FOR AN ORDINARY FACE

Wouldn't it be awful to have been born with a face so disfigured that when people looked at you for the first time they would turn away? Others, less thoughtful and more unkind, might even snicker and make fun, and this is very cruel. How devastating it must be to be ridiculed for something that wasn't your fault! If this had happened to you, could you have handled it?

Most of us have a face that might not win a prize in a beauty contest, but at least all the features of a normal human face are there and are shaped and positioned in the ordinary way. Someone has suggested that God must have loved ordinary people; that's the reason He made so many of them. Thank God for an ordinary face!

There have been many people born into our world with mishapen faces; it happens quite frequently. We are told that Charles William Eliot was one of these unfortunate ones. He was born in 1834 into a socially prominent family, but his face was seriously disfigured. This was before the miracles of modern plastic surgery. He had been examined by many of the finest surgeons of that day. The answer they all gave privately to his parents was that nothing could be done to improve his face. He would have to go through life with it as it was.

After many such consultations, his mother broke the news to him. What a devastating blow this must have been to him! It must have been the dark hour of his soul. Fortunately, his mother was a very caring, loving, and wise woman, and must have thought long and hard as to what words to use. It is reported that this is what she said: "My son, it is not possible for you to get rid of this handicap. We have consulted the best surgeons, and they say that nothing can be done. But it is possible for you, with God's help, to grow a mind and soul so big that people will forget to look at your face."

And he did exactly that! He grew a mind and soul so big that people forgot to look at his face. When he was graduated from high school, he was second in his class. He then entered Harvard University, from which he was graduated. At the age of thirty-five, he was selected to be its twenty-second president. He held this position for forty years.

He believed in the education and development of the soul as well as the mind. He did much to shape the course of American secondary education. He made the statement that a "five-foot shelf of books, designed to supply a broad literary background to those who were not college trained, if seriously and carefully studied, might supply a liberal education." A year after he retired as Harvard's president, he selected the fifty books which became known as "Dr. Eliot's Five-foot Shelf of Books." Today we know them as the Harvard Classics. He grew a mind and soul so big that people forgot to look at his face.

The next time, and every time, you look into a mirror, thank God for your face. It may be ordinary, but there isn't another one exactly like it in the whole world.

27

93-9-26.

PUTTING SHOES ON A GOOSE

"Stand firm then ... with your feet fitted with the readiness that comes from the gospel of peace" (Ephesians 6:15).

Paul spent a good bit of time in prison for preaching the gospel. While there, he had plenty of opportunity to notice the Roman soldiers and their equipment. This gave him an idea as he wrote to the Ephesians. "Put on the full armor of God," he wrote, and he compared the soldier's defenses with those of the Christian.

Interestingly, even the feet were included. The shoes of the soldier were then, as now, important to the soldier's ability to stand his ground. In fact, shoes are important to anyone who wants to be at his best at whatever he does.

Construction workers are often required to wear steel-toed shoes to protect their feet in case something heavy should fall on them. Men who work in the logging industry wear either hobnails or spikes on the soles of their shoes so that they will not slip when they walk on the logs. Some people wear shoes with metal cleats in the soles and heels to make them wear longer and evenly. Many shoes even have a metal arch support built into them for people who need extra support.

Good shoes are important to all of us. You probably have more than one pair of shoes. If you do, no doubt there is one pair that is your favorite, the one in which you feel your best. You would say they do the most for you, even though they might not be the best-looking of all the shoes you own. It's very difficult to do a good job of anything if your feet don't feel good.

Comfortable shoes have something to do with our feeling of self-respect and self-worth. Let me share with you a little secret. Whenever you have a very important social engagement, or when you are going for a job interview, or you have to stand before a group of people and give a speech or lead a discussion, always wear your favorite shoes, provided their color fits the rest of your outfit. It will give you confidence and courage, and you will be more apt to succeed because you feel good about yourself and what you are wearing.

Here is a story of how a farmer put shoes on a flock of geese. He was going to sell them to a poultry market in the city several miles away. He had no truck to get them there; so they were all going to have to walk. The only road to town was surfaced with fine crushed rock, and these little rocks were sharp and would cut the feet of the geese. Most everyone knows that the foot of a goose or duck is made like a paddle. It is specially designed for walking on dirt or grass, and for swimming, but not for walking mile upon mile over crushed rock. The farmer realized that if he drove them over this road, they would all be limping before they got to town because their feet would be all chewed up and bleeding. If they were delivered to the market in such a sorry and damaged condition, they would not bring the highest price.

He thought many days about how to overcome the problem and finally hit upon a tremendous idea. He cleaned the floor of one of the pens and poured warm, melted tar on it. He then drove the geese into this pen and let them walk around long enough for the bottoms of their feet to become coated with tar. Then he lifted each one to an adjoining pen, which had a floor covered with clean, dry sand. As they walked on the sand, the melted tar picked up a good thick layer of sand as it cooled. Wasn't that a clever idea? Now each goose was equipped with a pair of road shoes. He had an extra sole on the bottom of his paddles. So off to town they went, and the farmer received the top price for his flock of geese that day.

Just because we, as Christians, are God's chosen people does not mean that He is going to protect and shield us from all difficulties, trials, and tough going. He will not keep us from the difficult way, but will give us strength that will enable us to come out on the winning side even though the victory might be only within us. As we live and share the gospel, we can feel good about ourselves in spite of external circumstances. We can hold our ground against Satan. "Stand firm then . . . with your feet fitted with the readiness that comes from the gospel of peace."

NOT ALL ACCIDENTS ARE BAD

"What has happened to me has really served to advance the gospel" (Philippians 1:12).

Ivory Soap, as we know it today, is partly the result of an accident!

During the Civil War (1861-1865), the firm of Proctor and Gamble of Cincinnati, Ohio, had a contract to furnish candles and soap for the Army. They had so many orders that they had to run their little factory twenty-four hours a day and build machines which helped them produce more soap in less time. Then one day, something happened. One story says that during a night shift, a mixing-machine operator fell asleep on the job, and the machine overwhipped the mixture. The batch of soap was so overwhipped and contained so much air that the bars of soap floated when placed in water.

The foreman was about to have it dumped back into the kettle to be boiled again, but someone suggested, "Let's see; maybe the customers will like it." And they did! Soon, up and down the Ohio River, orders poured in, "Send us more floating soap."

For several years, it was known as "white" soap; then one Sunday in 1879, Harley Proctor, the company's first advertising and sales manager, found a better name for it when he heard the words of Psalm 45:8 in church: "All thy garments smell of myrrh and aloes and cassia out of ivory palaces...." He named his soap "Ivory." The first case of *Ivory Soap* was sold in October of that year.

Samples of this floating soap were sent to colleges and laboratories to be analyzed and compared with castile soaps, which were the finest soaps manufactured in that day. One chemist reported *Ivory Soap* to be "99 and 44/100% pure." These were magic words for advertising to Harley Proctor. Soon they were registered as the company's trademark with the U.S. Patent Office. "It Floats" was added in 1891 to make one of America's top advertising slogans of all time. And all this came to be because of an accident!

During his life as a Christian missionary, many "bad" things happened to the apostle Paul. Many times he got into trouble with the authorities; he was tried before rulers; he was put in prison; he was driven out of towns and forbidden to preach. One would think that all these bad things would slow down the progress of the gospel. But Paul believed that God was always in control and that for everything bad that happened, God could make good come of it.

And so it was. When he wrote to the Philippians, from a Roman prison, he could tell them God had used his problems to advance the gospel.

God is still in control today. He can take our bad experiences and work good, too. That's a great promise we can count on.

A QUESTION OF CONTROL

When a young concert violinist was touring Europe, the music critics exhausted their store of complimentary words in praising his musical ability. Many even went so far as to refer to him as "the world's greatest living violinist."

However, his initial concert in Great Britain was marred by an advance word in the column of an overcautious, caustic, and sarcastic critic who reported that "a large crowd is expected to hear the young artist. It is safe to assume that most of his hearers will be present to hear his $100,000 Stradivarius violin, rather than the young artist." Some people might have put some faith in the critic's remark. It also happened that the violinist had read the remark in the column.

Thousands were in attendance at his first concert in Britain. His audience sat spellbound as he played his first number. At its conclusion they literally rattled the rafters with their applause. As he bowed and bowed and bowed to acknowledge their enthusiasm and admiration of his artistry, he suddenly stunned them to silence by smashing the instrument over his knee. He then explained to his gasping and horrified hearers, "Now that I have played my first number on a cheap violin which I purchased this afternoon from a pawn shop for a few dollars, I will continue my concert with my Stradivarius."

The critic was wrong. It was not so much the instrument but the man who held the bow and did the playing that was important.

Each one of us ought to be as good an instrument as possible. But our real value is found in the Master's hand. There is much we cannot do, but we should never underestimate what God can do with us.

IT'S ALL
IN WHAT YOU DO WITH IT

Yussef and Ahmed were two young men who lived in the Orient. They sat for long hours, day after day, weaving tapestries for their master. Each morning they were given a supply of yarn for the day. Some of it was beautifully colored to represent the more pleasant emotions, while there were also the dark and dismal threads that represented the unpleasant emotions.

One day the allotment of yarn delivered to both of them contained a large heap of the black yarn of sorrow. Yussef was discouraged by such a stark and forbidding color. To show his displeasure, he wove the black threads into his pattern in harsh patches. Ahmed, on the other hand, used his allotment of black yarn in a different way. He wove it into his design with understanding and sympathy. In the yarn that had been delivered to them, there were also the gold threads of happiness, the purple threads of pain, and the blue threads of discouragement. Yussef did not bother to use any of them. The colors that he did choose, he shot with bitterness into his pattern, while Ahmed, with bold artistry, skillfully blended his allotment of precious threads with care and tenderness into the pattern as he worked.

When the master came to inspect their tapestries, Yussef growled that he had not been given the proper yarn. His tapestry was mediocre, almost worthless. But when the master examined Ahmed's work, he found it to be a masterpiece of the weaver's art because he had mingled light with shadow. Then the master gently said to the two craftsmen: "Both of you had the same materials, and you used them as you chose. It is not what comes to your life that determines the pattern, but the use you make of it."

As we go through life, we cannot escape trials, troubles, disappointments, sickness, temptation, reverses, and a host of other challenges along the way. These come to everyone. It is what we do about and with them that determines the pattern and design of our lives.

ACRES OF DIAMONDS

Dr. Russell Conwell, a Baptist minister of a few generations ago, developed a lecture that became very famous. He preached it hundreds of times. The title of the message was "Acres of Diamonds." It is the story of Ali Hafed, a Persian farmer who lived near the Indus River.

One day Ali Hafed was talking with a Buddhist priest, who told him about diamonds and how wealthy one could become if he possessed diamonds. Quite naturally, Ali Hafed was intrigued with the idea of going out into the world to find his fortune in diamonds. When he inquired of the priest where diamonds could be found, he was told, "You will find diamonds where a river flows over white sands between two high mountains. In those sands, there are diamonds."

So much did he want to become rich that in a matter of a few days Ali Hafed had sold his farm, got all his money together, and asked a neighbor to look after his family. He then set out in search of diamonds. He travelled all over the then-known world, from the mountains of the Moon to the corners of Europe. But Ali Hafed found no diamonds.

Eventually, his money was all gone; his clothes were in tatters; he was wretched and poor and miserable. One day, as he stood on the shore of the Bay of Barcelona in Spain, he could not resist the temptation to throw himself into the surf. He sank beneath the surface and was never seen again.

Meanwhile, the man who had purchased his farm was one day watering his camel in the garden. As the camel nosed about in the water of the shallow brook, the new owner saw a strange flash of light from the white sands of the stream. The man scooped up a milky white stone, carefully examined it, and then took it into his house. Later it was discovered that the stone was a diamond. The man who had purchased Ali Hafed's farm became wealthy beyond words because his farm became the site of the diamond mine of Golconda, one of the greatest diamond mines in history!

If only Ali Hafed had stayed at home and looked for diamonds in the white sands of the brook that flowed through his garden, he would have had acres of diamonds instead of poverty, starvation, and death by suicide.

We may often be tempted to believe that others have more reasons to enjoy life than we do. We can become so busy envying others that we lose sight of God's goodness to us and fail to use what we are and have to His glory. It is better to accept what we have and thank God for it than to complain and keep hoping for what we do not have. It's a good idea to make the most of what you have, who you are, and where you are. There may be some diamonds very close by.

THAT'S WHY I'M A VERY REMARKABLE FELLOW

William L. Stidger

Seventh Heaven is one of the truly great movies. If you ever get a chance to see it, don't miss it! It was first released many years ago as a silent picture and later with sound. One of the most unforgettable scenes in the story pictures Chico, who is the hero of the story, and the rat down in the dirty sewers beneath the streets of Paris. Chico works there. Suddenly a great gush of water poured from a manhole above and swept the rat into the river of vile smelling sewage. The rat might have drowned had not Chico rescued him. As the rat sat on the ledge drying himself, Chico unloaded some of his wholesome philosophy of life as he said, "I work in the sewers, Rat, but I live in the stars." Then he gave the rat some good advice: "Never look down! Always look up! I never look down! I always look up! That's why I'm a very remarkable fellow."

The rat cocked his head and listened carefully as though he understood every word. After all, wasn't Chico a very important person? Hadn't he just saved him from almost certain death? Chico continued his lecture and concluded with the words: "For those who will climb it, Rat, there is a ladder which leads from the sewer to the stars! And as you climb, Fellow, keep looking up! I always look up! I never look down! That's why I'm a very remarkable fellow!"

Chico's philosophy worked for him, as it will work for us. As the story continues, he climbed from the sewer to the street level of life; and then to a life of love, which was Seventh Heaven. I think that all of us have a bit of Chico in us. Maybe he was echoing something the Psalmist said many years ago in Psalm 121:1, "I lift up my eyes." Keep looking up!

Adapted from *There Are Sermons in Stories,* by William L. Stidger.

LEND A HELPING HAND

The apostle Paul had real problems in dealing with the church at Corinth. There were many things wrong in that fellowship, as there are bound to be things wrong in any church made up of imperfect people.

One of their difficulties was the mistake of wrong emphasis. In 1 Corinthians, the twelfth chapter, Paul mentioned more than a score of "gifts of the Spirit"—special abilities given to people to perform certain tasks, such as teaching, preaching, healing, working miracles, administering, speaking in tongues, and others. Many of these people felt that the gift of tongues was the greatest of all the gifts. To them, tongues was the "in" thing, and if you didn't have that gift, you were spiritually poor and unblessed. It is true that on the day of Pentecost, the gift of tongues was given to the disciples so that they could speak and be understood in languages they had never learned (Acts 2:7-8). This was a wonderful miracle that greatly helped the church get started, but it wasn't the only—or even the best—gift for God's service.

Leighton Ford tells the story of a seminary student who had met a Christian airline pilot who seemed to be very unhappy in his Christian experience. The pilot was a Christian, and had the assurance of salvation, but he was miserable because he had never been able to lead anyone to Christ. He said, "I have witnessed to other pilots; I have shared my faith with mechanics, flight attendants, and even supervisors, but I have not succeeded with a single one; it even seems that now no one wants to fly with me."

"It would appear that you don't have the gift of being an evangelist," said the student.

"What did you say?" queried the pilot. So the student repeated what he had said and tried to explain what he meant.

"No, I certainly don't have that gift," the pilot responded.

"What spiritual gift do you have?" inquired the student. After a few more questions and answers on spiritual gifts, the pilot summed up his capabilities in this way:

"Down at the church where I am a member, there always seem to be things that need fixing: a window gets broken, a door needs new hinges, rooms need to be repainted, and on and on, always something. It seems like most of the people down there aren't very practical about things like this, or they don't want to be, or don't have time. I have lots of spare time in my job, I have a great deal of know-how, and I just enjoy doing things like that."

The student then said, "You have a very important gift, the gift of helps. It's a gift that every church needs very much. I'm going to be in this city for several years getting my seminary training. Would you like for me to call you every time I hear of a need that you could take care of? Whether you respond to it yourself or pass it on to someone else doesn't make any difference."

The pilot agreed that he would, and as the months came and went, many special needs were referred to him. Practically all of them were taken care of by him or by someone he had recruited for the job. Not only did a great many good things get done that needed doing, but this pilot became as happy a Christian as you might ever meet.

God does not give the same gifts to all Christians. The gift of helps may not be as showy or as brilliant as a peacock, but it certainly is needed, and its exercise gets a lot of practical things accomplished.

Adapted from *Good News Is for Sharing,* by Leighton Ford, pp. 80-81.

BE GLAD YOU CAN FORGET

An ancient legend tells about a man who traveled over the countryside carrying two sacks; one hung down the front of him, and in it he carried the sins of people he knew. He wanted to have them where he could see them all the time and congratulate himself that he was not like them. The other sack was on his back, and in this he put all the good deeds of his friends, where he would not see them and he would soon forget them.

One day he met another man who also carried two sacks. Going up to him, and poking at the front sack, he asked what was in it. "Please stop punching," cried the man. "Those are my good deeds. I keep them out in front where I can always see them. Let me show you some of them: here is the money I put into the offering plate last Sunday. Here are some old clothes I recently gave to a beggar. This is a pair of mittens I gave to a crippled lad, and this is a small coin I put into the organ grinder's cup." Proudly he displayed all his good deeds.

"And what do you have in the sack on your back?"

"Tsk. Tsk. I don't want to look at anything that's back there. Those are my mistakes; that's why they are behind me."

"It appears that your sack of mistakes has more in it than your bag of good deeds." A frown clouded his face because he didn't want to be reminded that his mistakes outnumbered his good deeds. He was about to return an angry reply when another man stepped up, and lo, he, too, was carrying two sacks.

"What are you carrying in your sacks; may we see your cargo?" they inquired together.

"Gladly," replied the newcomer. "The bag in front is filled with the good deeds of others."

"It must be very heavy," remarked one man. "It looks as though it's almost full."

"And so it is," he replied. "But the weight of it is like sails to a ship or wings to an eagle. It encourages me and helps me on. There are so many good and wonderful people in the world."

"That sack on your back appears to be empty; it has holes in the bottom of it," said one of the men.

39

"Well, there's a good reason for that; I had a purpose in cutting those holes," answered the newcomer. "All the bad things I hear about people, I put in that sack and, sure enough, eventually they fall through the holes and are lost. So, you see I have nothing to drag me backward."

Which of these three men do you think carried the most pleasant load?

As we go through life, each one of us acquires a great deal of mental cargo having to do with the deeds and misdeeds of ourselves and others. Much of it is garbage and has no value for the future. One of the most important decisions we will make toward wholeness in our lives is deciding where we will carry these things—either in front of us, where we will constantly be reminded of them, or behind us, where they can be forgotten.

In Philippians 3:13, 14 the apostle Paul tells us how he dealt with a part of this problem: "Forgetting what is behind . . . I press on." This was a major part of his philosophy of living. A poor memory can be a great blessing. Thank God that you can forget.

LISTEN CAREFULLY

"Consider carefully how you listen" (Luke 8:18).

The purpose of words is to communicate thoughts. But sometimes when we hear others talk, we get the wrong message because we are not listening carefully. Often we misinterpret the message because we did not hear all of it, particularly the words that went before the words we thought we heard. Let me illustrate.

One day, three ladies were visiting over the back fence. All of them had heard a fourth neighbor make a statement earlier in the day, but each one had got a different message.

Mrs. Jones insisted that their friend had been to the zoo, because, said she, "I heard her mention a 'trained deer.'"

"I'm certain they were talking about going on a trip, because she said to her husband, 'Find out about the train, Dear.'" That's what Mrs. Smith heard.

Mrs. Young had heard still a different message. "I'm sure both of you are wrong. They must have been talking about music, because she definitely mentioned a 'trained ear.'"

About this time the neighbor who had made the statement suddenly appeared. The three ladies laughed as they told her of their disagreement. "Well," she said laughingly, "that's funny. All of you are poor guessers—or maybe poor hearers. You see, I had stayed overnight in the country, and when I came home, I asked my husband if it 'rained here' last night."

LET GEORGE DO IT

A wrecking crew had worked for more than two hours trying to get a railroad car back on the track. When the task was finally completed, young George Westinghouse, who had been observing the operation, said to a friend standing beside him, "That was a poorly handled job."

"It was tedious," the friend admitted, "but I don't see how they could have done it easier or better."

"There was an easier and better way that it could have been done," George told his friend. Then he went on to explain what he would have done and what kind of equipment he would have used. "It wouldn't be a bad idea for a railroad company to put together such a car replacer on the principle I have described, and have it on hand for use in emergencies," he told his friend.

The other man chuckled, "Why don't you make one?"

"I'll do it!" said George. And he did!

For the rest of his life, whenever George Westinghouse was challenged with a problem that everyone else had abandoned as hopeless, his answer was always, "I'll do it." Eventually, whenever George was around, everyone began to take the easy way out of a problem. They just decided to "let George do it."

He met his greatest challenge one day when he read of two passenger trains meeting in a head-on collision. The engineers of the wrecked trains had seen one another when yet a long way apart, but they could not stop in time because of the antiquated, simple, impracticable chain brakes with which each car was equipped.

"A brake is needed that will stop even the heaviest train within a few seconds," George told his friends. "I must devise such a mechanism." He tried dozens of methods—but they all failed. But each failure served merely to renew his determination. He had decided to do it, and do it he would!

One day he read of a compressed air drill that had been operated successfully by squeezing common air into an area one-sixth of its normal size, then releasing it all at once in the desired direction.

George snapped his fingers. "I've got it!" he cried. "If compressed air can run a drill, it can also stop a train." So in 1869, he invented the airbrake.

He came through again when he devised air springs to make motor travel more pleasant; and again when he underbid Edison himself and lit the 1893 World's Columbian Exposition in Chicago with a new kind of lamp.

Why is it that when improvement is called for in getting a job done, or someone must put in some time and energy to solve a problem to accomplish a task, we too often shrug our shoulders and "let George do it"? How fortunate it is for humanity that we are occasionally blessed with a George Westinghouse, with his ability to recognize a problem and then solve it.

Let's try to be like that!

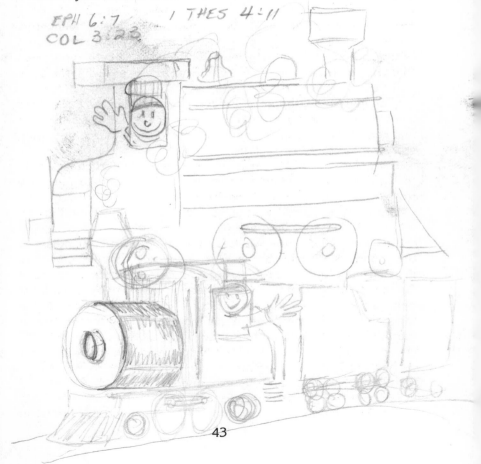

EPH 6:7   1 THES 4:11
COL 3:23

WITHOUT WAX ✓

Many words that we use every day have been in our language for generations. Some of them are as old as the language itself. Because language is a growing thing, there are some words that are as young as a little child, such as words that have to do with telecommunications, atomic energy, modern medicine, and computers.

Some words have a history of being born out of another language. The word *sincere* is an example. What do we mean when we use it? It is defined as "pure, genuine, frank, honest, true, unmixed, or unvarnished." When we sign a letter, "Sincerely yours," we mean that we have written a frank and honest letter. When you say, "I like him because he is always sincere," you mean that you can trust a person to be himself and to say what he really believes.

In all likelihood, the word "sincere" comes from the Latin word *sincerus,* which probably is a merging of two Latin words: *Sine* and *cera,* which mean "without wax." And there is an interesting story behind these two words.

The ancient Romans carried on business very much as we do today. There were many articles that they needed to purchase from someone else, such as benches, tables, stools, chests, chairs, cooking utensils, art objects, and sometimes building materials, which might be made of granite or stone.

Just like us today, they wanted to obtain good merchandise for the money they paid. Some were even so particular that they insisted it be almost perfect. Now anyone who has ever made anything realizes that to make something nearly perfect is almost impossible. In the making of furniture, a tool may slip and gouge the wood, or the chisel might cut too deeply into the granite or marble and cut a nick in the surface. The clever craftsman could cover the imperfection by filling the gouge or nick with wax. After he had finished polishing the article, it might appear to be perfect. Only if it were carefully examined by a pair of very skillful eyes could the deception be discovered.

The Romans, just like us today, did not want to be fooled in what they bought, so when a contract was let for a piece of merchandise that was to be made to order, the purchaser might stipulate that it was to be "sine-cera"—without wax. The Romans made so much fuss about poor merchandise that their rulers made a law that said any article made without wax rubbed in to make it look better than it really was had a special right and could be labeled "sine-cera."

The Bible has a great deal to say about this quality. If we are honest and frank in our dealings and do not pretend to be something we are not, we have the honor of being called "sincere." That quality takes a great deal of care, patience, and hard work to earn. It's neither cheap nor easy.

LIVING LETTERS

"You yourselves are our letter, written on our hearts, known and read by everybody" (2 Corinthians 3:2).

Everyone of us who belongs to Christ is a witness either for or against our Lord and His family—the church. In our text for today, the apostle Paul reminds the members of the church at Corinth that the way they were living was either adding to or subtracting from the influence of the gospel in their area. The same is also true of us. What a responsibility! We are either working for or against the cause of Christ in our world, and we do that more by how we live than by what we say.

One Sunday evening a minister preached a sermon on the power of the gospel. He closed the service with an invitation for people to accept Christ as Savior and Lord and thereby give God a chance to do something for them. Among those who responded to the invitation was a wealthy and well-known woman of the community. She asked the minister's permission to speak to the congregation. "I want all of you to understand why I came forward tonight," she said. "I accepted the invitation, not because of the fine sermon the minister preached, but because of the quiet influence of a wonderful Christian lady who is a member of your church and has been my housekeeper for many years. She is neither great nor famous, as the world uses those terms. She has lived Christianity in my home. I have never known her to lose her patience or to speak an unkind word to or about anyone. As far as I know, she has never done anything that was dishonorable. Her life is full of many little acts of unselfish love. There were times when I made fun of her faith. But when my little daughter died, she cried with me and helped me see beyond the grave and to shed my first tears of hope. Her life has been like a magnet drawing me to Christ, and I came forward this evening to get for myself that which makes her life so beautiful."

As the minister introduced the housekeeper to the congregation, he remarked: "Let me introduce to you the real preacher of the evening."

We may not have any of the showy gifts that would make us able to testify or sing or preach or teach, but the way we live our lives is a silent witness either for or against our Lord. The best sermons in the world are found in boots—not in books. We are Christ's letter to the world. They may never read our Bible, but they do read us.

"We are the only Bibles the careless world will read;
We are the sinner's gospel; we are the scoffer's creed;
We are the Lord's last message, given in deed and word;
What if the type is crooked; what if the print is blurred?"
—*Anonymous*

HUSH PUPPIES Acts 11:26

If a person calls himself a Christian, what qualities would you expect to find in his life? We expect a Christian to be someone who has truly taken Christ as Savior and is trying to follow Him as Lord of his life. Such qualities as being loving, forgiving, caring, patient, and generous are some of the evidences we would expect to find in a Christian's life. People associate Christians with Christ, and they have a right to do that. We are supposed to be examples of what Christ can do with a person's life.

What comes to your mind when I mention the trademark *Hush Puppies?* Shoes—that's right. In a recent survey, 97% of the adults who were asked knew that *Hush Puppies* had something to do with shoes. The word has got around.

But do you know why they are called *Hush Puppies?* It happened somewhat by accident. Long before 1957, a company by the name of Wolverine Worldwide manufactured leather goods such as gloves, handbags, and hats—most of them made from pigskin. In 1957, they began manufacturing a pigskin shoe that provided a great deal of casual comfort, but they could not think of a name for it. Then one day, the sales manager took a pair to show to a customer in Tennessee. After the family had entertained him at dinner in their home, the host picked up a plate of left-over fried corn meal mush, took it outside, and fed it to the dogs, which had been barking continuously while they were having dinner. When the sales manager inquired about what it was he had fed the dogs, he explained: "Whenever we feed the dogs the cornmeal, they quit barking; so we call it 'hush puppies.'"

"Eureka," thought the salesman. "Many people in our country call their feet 'dogs,' and sometimes when our feet hurt badly, we say, 'My dogs are really barking!'"

So, in order to keep your dogs from barking, you wear a pair of soft *Hush Puppies.* The name really stands for a special kind of foot comfort.

As people watch you and me live, feel, and act, are they always reminded of the qualities the world found in Jesus Christ? How important it is to live up to our calling!

LIVING WELL
IS A FULL-TIME JOB

I believe this story comes from Holland. The lesson it teaches, however, applies to people of all countries of the world.

Someone once asked an old man how or why it was that by the time evening came, he was always so tired. The old man answered: "That's because I am so busy all day. I have to train two falcons. I must watch two hares so they will not escape. I have to teach two hawks not to be greedy. A snake has to be tamed. I have to keep a lion well under control. And last, but not least, I have to keep an eye on a sick old man."

"Well," said the friend, "I know you don't work in a zoo; you must be joking then, because no one can do so many things in one day. Tell me what you mean."

"Yes," said the old man. "It is the truth. The falcons are my eyes. I have to train them all the time, so that they are used only for those things that bring me happiness. The two hares are my feet. I have to guide them to go along the good path. The two hawks are my hands. I have to learn to use them for useful works, like supporting those who are in need as well as myself. The snake is my tongue. I have to watch it all the time in being careful what I say, and certainly not to use it in gossiping. The lion is my heart. I always have to battle with it. This is the center of my being and sometimes wants to take complete control of me and things and other people, when I should be always depending on the grace and will of God for my life. The sick old man is my entire body. I always have to watch it so that my thoughts and actions bring honor to the Lord."

THE PLIMSOLL LINE

About the middle of the eighteen hundreds, Samuel Plimsoll, a London coal dealer, became interested in some of the evil practices among those who owned and operated merchant ships. These ships carried cargo all over the world, but there were very few safety regulations in those days. Many ships put out to sea dangerously overloaded. Others were old and unseaworthy, too fragile to ride through heavy seas. Still others were undermanned. These were called "coffin ships," because many sailors went to the bottom of the ocean with them. Many of these ships were so overinsured that if they did sink, their owners would pocket more money than if they had arrived safely at their destinations.

Samuel Plimsoll was elected to Parliament in 1868. Immediately he set about plans for the revision of commercial shipping laws. Because of his interest and influence, Parliament enacted the Merchant Shipping Act in 1876. As a result of his efforts, he became known as the sailor's friend, because safety measures that resulted from this act prevented many disasters at sea and saved thousands of lives.

One of the provisions of this act required that every ship must have a visible line fixing the limits to which it could be loaded. In the beginning, this line was painted amidships on both the port and starboard sides. It consisted of a circle, twelve inches in diameter with a horizontal line eighteen inches long through the circle.

This became known as the Plimsoll line, and it is affixed to all merchant vessels. It indicates the depth a ship can be submerged in the water and still be safe in a storm. Engineers can calculate how much cargo a vessel can safely carry and how deep the hull will ride in the water when it is fully loaded. The Plimsoll line is placed at this waterline. It tells those who are loading the ship that this is as far as they can go. They are not to load it beyond this point.

Some people think that there are some temptations so powerful that they will conquer you no matter what. Don't you believe it! Satan does not have the power to overload you with tempta-tions so that you will surely yield. He has no such arrow in his quiver. He is not all-powerful, and that is the reason he has such a disappointing time with some people. He is unable to get them to do what he wants them to do because they are so whole-hearted in following Christ. He can't get an arrow in anywhere because they are wearing the whole armor of God (Ephesians 6:13 ff). Their strength can be compared to the strength of a modern war tank in withstanding the darts, arrows, and spears of primitive warriors.

God permits us to be tempted for our own good, but we have His Word on this: "God is faithful; he will not let you to be tempted beyond what you can bear. But when you are tempted, he will also provide a way out so that you can stand up under it" (1 Corinthians 10:13).

For each one of us there is a fixed point. Satan will never be able to tempt us beyond what we can bear. God made that law, and He will see that it is enforced until the end of time!

GATOR AID

One of the soft drinks on the market today is *Gatorade.* It is a good-tasting and refreshing drink indeed. From the advertising we see on it, it is highly recommended to athletes as having the right ingredients to help make one a winner. It's supposed to replace body minerals and provide the extra bit of energy one needs to put him in the lead.

Now, I don't know who gave it the name *Gatorade,* but it might have been born in a military training camp in Florida during World War II days. Everyone in the military knows the value of discipline and hardship in the development of a good soldier. In this particular camp, the daily training featured a long run and a difficult and grueling obstacle course. On the last stretch of this course, recruits had to grab a rope suspended from above, swing across a shallow pool of water, and drop to the ground on the other side. The weather in Florida is sometimes hot and humid, and that made the pond very much a temptation. It seemed that many of the recruits just seemed to drop their hot and sweaty bodies right in the middle of the pool instead of making it all the way across.

One day their lieutenant, who was more clever than some of his troops, made the pool the new home for a gigantic alligator. Guess what? After that, every recruit fell in the dust well beyond the edge of the pool. You see, the gator gave them that extra aid that got them well on the other side—Gator Aid.

Sometimes we are encouraged to do the right thing because we are afraid of, or would not want the result of, doing the wrong thing. The recruits did not want to swim in the same pool with the alligator. When it is raining, we may wear overshoes or boots, a raincoat, and carry an umbrella because we don't want to catch a cold. We acquire an education because we don't want to remain ignorant. We brush our teeth several times each day because we don't like bad check-ups or the dentist's drill. We eat properly and exercise regularly because we don't want to become a candidate for heart disease. We drive our cars on the highway defensively and sometimes even courteously by not always exercising our rights because we want to be a survivor rather than a statistic. And on and on we could go. We don't want the bad result; so we alter our course and stay out of harm's way.

A long time ago, the psalmist said: "It is good for me to be afflicted so that I might learn your decrees" (Psalm 119:71). Afflictions and difficult circumstances are not easy for anyone, but without them, we could not expect to become spiritually strong and enduring. If all of life were as easy as coasting down a hill, we would never know the thrill that comes from climbing a mountain.

JESUS AND THE COLT √

Scripture Text: Luke 19:30-38

As easy and natural as it seems, riding a horse is not a natural event. What's natural for a horse is what goes on at rodeos in the bucking bronc and bull-riding events. Without being "broken," an animal simply does not tolerate having a human on its back.

Breaking a horse is a dangerous practice, but it must be done if the horse is to be of any value. If the horse has been raised around people, the job is much easier. The horse has learned to trust people, and he can be broken at an early age, before he reaches his full strength.

It's a different story with a wild horse, and extra precautions must be taken. The horse is afraid of people, and believes they are trying to hurt him. He fights with all his might to resist them.

I am told that sometime before the horse is to be broken, a saddle is strapped to his back and left there for several hours at a time and a few days in succession. In this way, he becomes accustomed to having something on his back. Even though he may buck and kick a great deal at the beginning, he soon becomes used to its being there, and he accepts it.

In addition to the saddle, a bridle is buckled onto his head. This bridle has an iron bit that is placed cross-wise in the horse's mouth and behind his back teeth. This does not hurt the horse. To the ends of this bit, which stick out about an inch on each side of the horse's mouth, the rein is fastened. The rider holds this rein in his hands to guide, restrain, or control the horse. When the rider pulls on the rein, the horse experiences some discomfort to his mouth. If the rider pulls to the right, the horse's head turns to the right, and he shifts his body to go in that direction. In being ridden, the horse soon learns to follow the pull of the rein because it hurts less that way. This is how he learns what it means to obey his master.

But on the day of the breaking, it's a different matter entirely. With the saddle on his back, the bridle on his head, and the rein over his neck, the horse is ready for the cowboy to break him. The horse is driven into a chute—a narrow path between two high fences, so narrow that the horse cannot turn around and run away, although that is what he would like to do. To a horse in this situation, there's only one way to go, and that's forward!

Now the rider gets onto the saddle. The gate is opened, and away they go. The horse kicks, bucks, and squeals all over the arena. He has only one thing in mind, and that is to spill the rider in the dust. But the experienced cowboy stays with him (at least in most instances) until the poor critter is worn out, exhausted, and frothing all over his body with a foamy, lathery sweat. By this time he's had it. He now accepts his master. Of course, it will take quite a while for him to become as gentle as a kitten, but usually he'll become so mild and refined that even a child may ride with safety.

In the story of the triumphal entry, Luke tells us that Jesus told two of His disciples to go into the village and bring back a colt of a donkey, which no one had ridden. This they did because He was their Master. Jesus mounted it and made His triumphal entry into Jerusalem, the Holy City. Now a donkey needs to be broken just as a horse does, but there was no kicking, bucking, or squealing on the part of the colt. Even in the midst of all the shouting of the mob and the waving of palm branches of those who lined the streets and pressed in on the Lord, the donkey colt was as tame as could be.

A cowboy once remarked about this incident that "Jesus must have had wonderful hands to pull it off so smoothly." I can imagine that when the colt was brought to our Lord, He probably patted it on the shoulder, stroked its long face with His gentle hands, and spoke to it in tones that were kind and soothing to the frightened little animal. Whatever it was, we can be sure that when Jesus took the reins, the colt recognized Him as the Master.

Many of the details of this story are also true of our lives. Whether we were born and brought up in a Christian home or out on the range of the world where we had no knowledge of who Jesus is, each one of us must come to that personal experience of accepting Him as the Master of our lives if we are ever to be a useful part of His kingdom. He wants to get His hands on each of us and use us, and it's much easier and better for us if we let Him become our Master while we are young. The older we get, the harder we are to "break." I don't know of any better hands in which you could trust your entire life.

A LONG CONSCIENCE

For many years, ships that were going to or from New York Harbor had to pass through the Narrows, a very narrow and dangerous channel sixteen miles long. Many ships were wrecked in this narrow bit of water. Every possible means of preventing such accidents had been tried—lighthouses erected along the way, bouys that tolled their bells twenty-four hours a day, and fog horns that sounded off their frightening warnings all seemed to no avail. Accidents continued to happen.

Then one day, an engineer suggested laying an electrical cable in the center of the channel, and sending an alternating current through it. Everything else had failed; so they decided to install the cable over the sixteen-mile route. That solved the problem.

The cable sends out sound waves that are picked up by audophones, similar to microphones, which are attached to the hull of the ship. These sound waves are transferred to the pilot's wheel-house. The skipper can tell by the sound when his ship is directly over the cable. It matters not how thick the fog, how black the night, or how treacherous the storm, the pilot can follow this cable in safety. The Narrows is now as safe as it can be made, so long as the ship has the equipment to pick up the signal and the pilot steers by it. One might say that the cable is the ship's conscience, and only by following it can the pilot steer his craft safely through the dangerous Narrows.

A modern airplane pilot uses a similar device when visual contact with his surroundings is impossible. It is called a "beam." The beam is a straight line between two points, the airport the plane is leaving and the one to which it is going. Instruments in the cockpit constantly inform the pilot where his aircraft is in relation to this electrical signal. When he is exactly on track, we say he is "on the beam."

A small child suggested that the conscience is a still, small voice that warns us when something is wrong. A conscience is a good thing, but it is not always safe to follow. In order for it to be a safe guide, it must be educated or tuned to the right principles of God's Word, and the principles of good living. If the cable had not

56

little voice we have to argue with.

been laid in the *center* of the Narrows, it would not have been a safe guide.

The apostle Paul's conscience was directed by the Holy Spirit, and he followed it; so he could say, "My conscience confirms it" (Romans 9:1). Some people do not have a reliable conscience because they push it before them as one pushes a wheelbarrow, and you can make a wheelbarrow go anywhere you want it to go. A person whose conscience never troubles him must have it well trained to suit his own purposes. When our conscience is tuned into God's laws, it is safe to follow. Keep in touch with it and follow it!

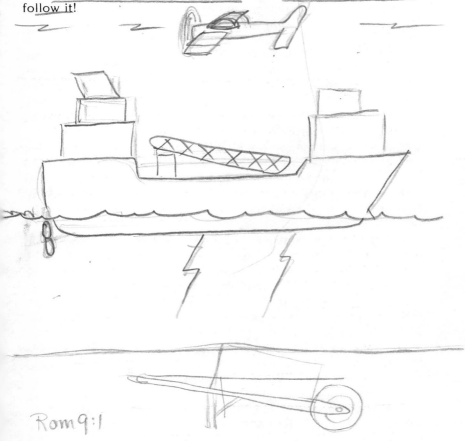

Rom 9:1

JESUS AND JUDAS

During the years that Leonardo daVinci was painting the Lord's Supper, he lived in Milan, Italy. Before he could paint the thirteen figures, it was necessary to find men who could serve as models. Each model had to have a face that expressed the artist's idea of the man he would represent. Doubtless, this was not an easy task.

One Sunday as he was worshiping in the cathedral, he saw a young man in the choir who looked as daVinci thought Christ would have looked. He had the features of love, tenderness, concern, innocence, compassion, interest, and kindness. Arrangements were made, and the young man sat as the model for our Lord.

Many months and even years went by, and the painting still was not finished. The artist had not yet found a model for Judas. He was looking for a man whose face showed wickedness, sin, greed, lust, and hopelessness. Ten years after he had painted the picture of Christ, he found a man in a Roman prison whose face seemed to have all the qualities of Judas that he had been looking for. Consent was given, and the man, Pietro Bandinelli, sat as the model for Judas.

The painter worked tirelessly for days. But as the work went on, a certain change seemed to come over the model. His face seemed to be filled with tension, and his bloodshot eyes were filled with horror as he looked upon the painted likeness of himself on the canvas. One day, Leonardo sensed the man's uneasiness so much that he paused in his work and asked, "My son, what troubles you so?"

The man buried his face in his hands and began to sob. After a long time he raised his head and asked, "Do you not remember me? Years ago I was your model for the Savior."

This unfortunate man, like the prodigal son, had turned his life over to Satan and the world and had been dragged down to the level of degradation. He no longer loved the things he had loved before. And those things that he at one time had hated and despised, now he loved. Where once there was love, now there was hate; where once there was hope, now there was despair.

THE WHITTLER
WHO BECAME FAMOUS

Salvator, Julio, and Antonio were three junior boys who lived in Cremona, Italy, about the middle of the 1600's. Julio played the violin and Salvator loved to sing as he played. Antonio also liked music and would have loved to sing, but he had such a squeaky voice that the children made fun of him when he tried. But Antonio was not without talent. His most precious possession was his pocketknife, and he was always whittling away on some piece of wood. He had made some very nice things with this talent.

It was festival time in the small city. The streets and the houses were beautifully decorated, and people wore their finest clothes and were having a joyous time. In those days, it was the custom for children to play musical instruments and sing on the street corners and in public places, especially at holiday times, and people would give them money to show their appreciation. On this particular day, Salvator and Julio were planning to go to the cathedral, where they would play and sing on the sidewalk as the people came and went.

"Would you like to go with us?" they called to Antonio, who stood nearby whittling on a piece of wood. "Maybe you can't sing, but we'd like to have you come anyway."

"Sure, I would like to come," he replied.

Soon they were on their way. As they walked along, Antonio kept thinking about the unkind remark about his not being able to sing. It made him cry in his heart, because he loved music, too, even though he couldn't sing.

When they arrived at the cathedral, Julio began to play while Salvator sang. People stopped to listen, and most of them left a coin or two for the shabbily dressed boys.

An elderly man stepped from the group of passersby and said to the boys, "That was a beautiful song; would you sing it again for a lonely, old man?"

"Certainly," said Salvator, and the boys repeated the number.

He complimented them again as he placed a coin in Salvator's hand, and soon he was lost in the crowd.

Salvator opened his hand and looked at the coin. "Look! A gold piece!" he shouted. All three boys had a part in holding the coin and examining it; they all agreed that it was a real gold coin.

"But he can well afford it," said Julio. "He's the great Amati."

"And who is Amati, and why is he great?" inquired Antonio.

Both boys laughed as they said, "You have never heard of Amati?"

"Of course, he hasn't" said Julio. "He knows nothing of music makers; he has only a squeaky voice and is just a whittler. For your information, Antonio, Amati is a great violin maker, probably the greatest in all Italy or even the world, and he lives in our city."

As Antonio walked home that evening, his heart was very heavy with sad thoughts. It seemed to him that he had been laughed at too long for his squeaky voice and his whittling.

Very early the next morning, Antonio left his home, carrying his precious pocketknife and his pockets filled with some of the things he had made. He was determined to find the great Amati.

Eventually, he found his house and gently knocked on the front door. Amati's servant came to the door and scoldingly asked: "Who are you; and what do you want here?"

Frightened and brokenhearted, Antonio turned away without even answering and walked slowly down the street. He sat down and waited until the sun was higher in the sky and then returned to the house and knocked again. This time, when the servant opened the door, the great master heard the boy's voice and came to see what he wanted.

"I brought these for you to see," said Antonio, as he held out some of the things he had carved. "I hope you will look at them and tell me whether I have enough talent to learn how to make violins."

The great master took the articles in his hands, carefully examined them, and then invited Antonio into the house.

"What is your name?" he asked.

"Antonio, sir," he replied. "Antonio Stradivari."

"And why do you want to make violins," inquired the master.

"Because I love music," replied Antonio, "but I cannot sing because of my squeaky voice. You heard my friends Salvator and Julio in front of the cathedral yesterday."

"The thing that matters the most is the song in the heart," said Mr. Amati. "There are many ways of making music: some people play the violin, others sing, still others paint pictures to express

60

their joy. Each helps to add to the loveliness of the world. You are a whittler, but your song shall be as noble as any." These words made Antonio very happy, and he never forgot them.

In a very short while, Antonio became a pupil of the great artist. Every morning, very early, he went to Mr. Amati's workshop, where he listened and learned and watched with Mr. Amati as his teacher. After many years, there was not one secret about the making of a violin, with all of its more than seventy pieces, that he did not know. By the time he was twenty-two years old, his master allowed him to put his own name on a violin he had made.

For the rest of his life, Antonio made violins—more than 1100 of them—trying to make each one better and more beautiful than the one before. In time, he became as famous as the master who had taught him. More than half of his violins are still in existence and are being played all over the world. Needless to say, they are very valuable. Anyone who owns a Stradivarius violin owns a treasure.

We may not be able to sing or play or make violins, but if we really want to, we will find a way to let the music out of our hearts and praise God with it.

WHAT IT TAKES TO SUCCEED

"... straining toward what is ahead, I press on toward the goal" (Philippians 3:13, 14).

Someone once asked Walt Disney for the secret of his success. This was his reply: "It was hard work, imagination, belief in myself, and incredible struggle."

As a boy, Walt Disney was a dreamer. He had many desires, and he loved to draw. Many of his boyhood hours were spent in dreaming and fantasizing. He saw romance in everything. Then he would try to put into pictures or cartoons the things he had seen in his mind. He wanted to be a cartoonist.

One day, he submitted some of his cartoons to an editor of a Kansas City newspaper. The editor rejected them with these words: "I advise you to give up trying to be a cartoonist, because it is easy to see from these drawings that you have no talent in that direction."

Although this was a bitter blow, Walt Disney did not walk out on his dream of being a cartoonist. He had a tremendous faith in his ability. He submitted his sketches to many other newspapers and studios—one after another—always to be rejected. But he did not give up. Finally, he found a job drawing publicity material for churches, probably at a mere pittance of a salary. But it was a beginning, and it gave him a chance to prove his ability to the world.

Now that he was an artist, he had to have a studio. He had no money, but after searching a long time, he found an old, mice-infested garage that was for rent at a very low price. Here Walt Disney dreamed his dreams and spun his fancies.

During these early years of his career in his "studio," he became well acquainted with one certain mouse that showed up several times every day just as though he was checking up on the young artist's progress. Disney became very fond of this little rodent and many times shared his lunch with it. As time went on, the mouse became quite tame and approachable, probably not to the point of being willing to be picked up and petted, but at least it was willing to come close to the master of the studio without being frightened. Walt Disney spent hours sitting at his desk and drawing board watching this mouse; he studied its every movement and response to whatever he did.

Thirty years later, Walt Disney was a famous man in the world of entertainment, and the character next to him in his fame was Mickey, the mouse. As a matter of fact, he became the most famous mouse in the whole world, and he probably will remain so for many years to come. Of course, we can assume that Mickey was born in a garage "studio," and Mr. Disney never forgot that he was born in his mind and dreams while he was working in his "studio."

You see, both of them had come into their tomorrows out of dark nights.

On one occasion, Mr. Disney said that the secret of success "is to trust God and to exercise your God-given imagination. It is to dream and to be willing to struggle."

That's good and sound advice for anyone, anytime!

More Books for
YOUTH and ADULTS

Skits That Teach, by Colleen Ison. Here are twelve skits to inspire self-examination. In each, Christians will be able to look at themselves for such faults as apathy, self-indulgence, lack of faith, and hypocrisy. There are also questions for discussion included. **#3356.**

Check Your Commitment: Studies in Matthew. Here are thirteen lessons from the gospel of Matthew that show what commitment to Christ really costs. Knofel Staton is not interested in religious platitudes and cliches. Some days are tough—even for Christians. They were for Jesus, too. Christianity is no easy way out—but it's the best way. And it takes commitment to walk it. Instructor's edition, **#39982;** student's, **#39983.**

A History of the English Bible. How do we know the Bible is reliable? What does *inspired* mean? Which translation should I use? If you've wondered about any of these questions, or if your young people need some reassurance of the Bible's relevance, this book will help. Starting with a unit on the nature of the Bible, Jonathan Underwood traces the development of the Bible from the original manuscripts to a variety of English translations. **#39974.**

Available at your Christian bookstore or

STANDARD PUBLISHING